APR 2 7 2009

OBAMA

THE HISTORIC CAMPAIGN IN PHOTOGRAPHS

OBAMA

THE HISTORIC CAMPAIGN IN PHOTOGRAPHS

DEBORAH WILLIS *and* KEVIN MERIDA

Amistad

An Imprint of HarperCollins*Publishers*

Portraits of candidates

and candid shots of their supporters and detractors have traditionally comprised nineteenth- and twentieth-century photography of presidential campaigns. Through the years, political photography has been used for a variety of purposes—from documenting a candidate's appeal by showcasing him or her amidst sizable crowds to highlighting their of-the-people appeal through pictures of them eating at mom-and-pop diners or holding babies. We also come to think of family portraits or childhood photos as ways of humanizing those who aspire to lead the free world. These kinds of images can be found in *Obama: The Historic Campaign in Photographs* and then some. Yet this collection also shows images of elements unique to Obama's historic campaign: teeming crowds more notably multiracial than any other campaign's in recent memory, the appeal to and inclusion of youth in the candidate's successful bid for the Democratic Party nomination, and the candidate's use of technology to build support, whether it be a photograph of Obama on a BlackBerry or an image of a campaign staffer who knew particularly well the power of the Internet.

Through 150 photographs, *Obama: The Historic Campaign in Photographs* highlights the road to Barack Obama's groundbreaking nomination as the first black American to lead the presidential ticket of a major party. The images are politically contextualized by the *Washington Post*'s Kevin Merida, who covered the campaign for the paper. His essay charts Obama's road to the nomination and places his achievement in the historical context of African American political advancement.

Photography has played a significant role in framing Obama, both as an icon and as a subject of curiosity. This unique collection documents the public and private moments of his campaign and includes photographs by professional photojournalists and portrait photographers as well as by volunteers, rallygoers, and young supporters who used their cell phones and video or digital cameras to capture his image. As a photohistorian, I decided to include images from amateur photographers because Obama's ability to connect with people of all ages and classes and their desire to preserve his likeness for posterity is essential to the story of his nomination. Their desire to cheer for him, to listen to his every word, to lionize and accord him respect as if he's already president, is palpable. As is traditional with presidential photography, whether he's being photographed by a professional or an amateur, the images, at times, look almost biblical. This is not a new trend. As indicated in Lonnie G. Bunch's *The American Presidency: A Glorious Burden:* "Presidents inhabit our collective memory in part because of an astonishing array of media.

Portraits, photographs, film, television, folk songs, Broadway musicals, advertisements, and souvenirs have all served to celebrate, criticize, satirize, sell, legitimize, exploit, praise, and memorialize the holder of this office."

I researched thousands of images—from picture agencies, individual photographers, and families who attended parties and campaign events. Many have a spirit of optimism and joy. Public interest in this book was encouraging as more and more photographs were given to me. Many people shared stories about the day they saw him or met him; one story was particularly memorable: Elise Jones Martin. Her son, Montez Martin, sent me a note and a photograph taken during Obama's visit to South Carolina and enthusiastically gave me permission to use it in this book; Merida discusses it as well (see page 117).

Rather than chronologically following the campaign from the initial announcement, the photographs are grouped thematically based on the subject, from intimate and personal shots of Barack Obama with his family to pictures of the candidate speaking to large crowds in grand public spaces. The book then moves on to images that show how Barack Obama is perceived as an iconic figure who is suspect, praised, and admired. Others show people using popular and material culture, including symbolic trinkets, mementos, T-shirts, and small gifts, such as JFK campaign buttons, a wristband honoring a deceased soldier, commemorative coins, and an Obama necklace made from pieces of a Scrabble game, to express their trust in the candidate. These collectibles reveal "much

Annie Leibovitz catches Obama in a contemplative pose, relaxed but in reflection, during a *Men's Vogue* photography session.

about changing notions of how a president can or should be remembered," as described in *The American Presidency: A Glorious Burden.*

Photographers have documented Obama in various candid poses, from talking to one of his daughters on a cell phone or buying a kaleidoscope for his children in a tourist gift shop to imposing and striking portraits of a leader standing high on a flag-draped platform, a handsome, dapperly dressed man who exudes high moral character or the everyman wearing a white shirt with and without a tie. Photographs of the Obama family waving to crowds or with the Kennedys, the Clintons, Oprah Winfrey, and other celebrities and anonymous families are interspersed throughout the book as well as photographs of political leaders and rivals, religious figures, educators, and young children whose faces and bodies are decorated with the Obama logo. There are also photographs of broadcast news coverage of the debates as well as on-camera images before and after press conferences. These documentary photographs transfer inspirational messages from Obama's campaign to the American public.

Michelle Obama—wife, mother, and executive administrator—appears smartly dressed and fashionably aware whether in evening attire or everyday dress. She is shown in this book expressing love and respect with humor and support. Hugging her husband with her arms around his back, she exemplifies beauty, strength, and encouragement in one of the series of "fist bump" images that reveal a sense of camaraderie between the two. Viewed outside the stereotypes presented in some broadcast and print news stories, Michelle Obama's photographs reveal that she is a highly poised woman who is prepared to take on the duties of First Lady.

Obama: The Historic Campaign in Photographs offers us a moment to pause and consider this campaign, one that instilled a sense of hope, joy, and dignity in unexpected places. The viewer will find ironic and iconic images that will shape the understanding of this landmark political season. The book also helps us understand how image and text are used in presidential campaigns. One revealing slogan shared the podium with Obama at a rally: Built to Last.

Since the beginning of photographic history, photographs of presidential campaigns have had a special connection to the viewer. They can be viewed as evidence of a unique moment in the viewer's history. This book shows us a unique moment in our national history. More, these images show not only the range of his supporters and how support escalated but also how photography was instrumental in galvanizing the public.

The broad array of images is transformative, as they express beauty, pathos, poignancy, emotion, and euphoria about the man Barack Obama and the presidential campaign.

—Deborah Willis

About the Author

Named one of the 100 Most Important People in Photography by *American Photography* magazine, Deborah Willis is department chair and professor of photography and imaging at the Tisch School of the Arts, New York University. A 2005 Guggenheim Fellow, a Fletcher Fellow, and a 2000 MacArthur Fellow, she is one of the nation's leading historians and curators of American photography. Some of her notable books include *The Black Female Body: A Photographic History*, with Carla Williams; *A Small Nation of People: W. E. B. Du Bois and the Photographs from the Paris Exposition*; *Reflections in Black: A History of Black Photographers, 1840 to the Present*; *Picturing Us: African American Identity in Photography*; and *VanDerZee: The Portraits of James VanDerZee*. She is also a photographer whose work has been exhibited throughout the United States. She lives in New York City.

Obama at his U.S. Senate office, oldest daughter, Malia, at his side, and youngest

daughter, Sasha, being held by his wife, Michelle. In the backdrop are photographs

of two men Obama admires: ABRAHAM LINCOLN and

MUHAMMAD ALI. Obama invoked Lincoln's faith against

impossible odds when he announced his candidacy on February 10, 2007.

And it was Ali, like Obama this campaign season, who shocked the world by

defeating the seemingly invincible Sonny Liston not once, but twice.

A GIDDY GROUP OF GIRLS flaunt their emotion by jumping off a seawall after an Obama rally on February 8, 2008, in Corpus Christi, Texas. Hillary Clinton kept her candidacy alive by winning the crucial Texas primary on March 4. But in the state's two-step process of awarding delegates, Obama won the Texas caucuses and ended up with more overall delegates, 99 to Clinton's 94.

Obama returns to his campaign bus on January 8, 2008, after thanking campaign volunteers at the Jewett Street School in Manchester, New Hampshire. After winning the Iowa caucuses, Obama was dealt a setback in New Hampshire.

Obama speaks to a group of supporters at the Farmers Public Market Building in Oklahoma City, Oklahoma, March 17, 2007.

During an Obama campaign stop at the Iowa State Fair, a supporter holds up

a *Newsweek* cover featuring the Democratic candidate, who takes notice.

———————

Opposite: Obama addresses supporters at a town-hall meeting at the Uni-

versity of New Hampshire in Durham, New Hampshire, February 12, 2007.

Obama greets supporters after former vice president Al Gore endorsed him at a rally at Joe Louis Arena in Detroit, June 16, 2008. Gore was the last big-name Democrat to throw his weight behind Obama, but by the time he did, the race was decided. Gore stayed neutral and mostly mum during the long Democratic contest, leading to speculation that he might help mediate an end to the nomination battle between Clinton and Obama or somehow emerge himself as the compromise choice at a brokered Democratic National Convention.

Opposite: Campaigning in Fairless Hills, Pennsylvania, Obama displays some of the lucky charms people gave him along the campaign trail. He keeps the assorted trinkets in his pocket.

Obama delivers a 2OO8 FATHER'S DAY SPEECH at Apostolic Church of God in Chicago, highlighting the importance of fathers being involved in the raising of their children. Obama's own Kenyan father, Barack Hussein Obama, Sr., abandoned him when the boy was two. The elder Obama left his wife and son behind in Hawaii to study at Harvard and never returned. He later remarried and moved back to Kenya, seeing young Barack (then known as Barry) only once more, during a December 1971 Christmas visit to Hawaii. Barry was ten then. Obama Sr. died in a car accident in 1982. His son has returned again and again to the subject of parental responsibility during his political career. The speech in Chicago, however, triggered a backlash from some African American notables, including Georgetown University professor Michael Eric Dyson and the Reverend Jesse Jackson. Both Dyson and Jackson are Obama supporters.

Obama waves to supporters during a rally that drew more than 10,000 at Nissan Pavilion in Bristow, Virginia. The rally was the key event in Obama's launch of his general-election campaign on June 5, 2008, two days after securing his party's nomination. That Obama chose VIRGINIA indicates the importance the campaign placed on the state, which a Democrat hadn't carried in the fall election since President Lyndon Johnson did it in 1964. Obama carried the Virginia primary, helped by the early support of his good friend Governor Tim Kaine.

A Native American woman in traditional clothing cheers on Obama at a rally at the Four Seasons Arena in Great Falls, Montana, May 30, 2008.

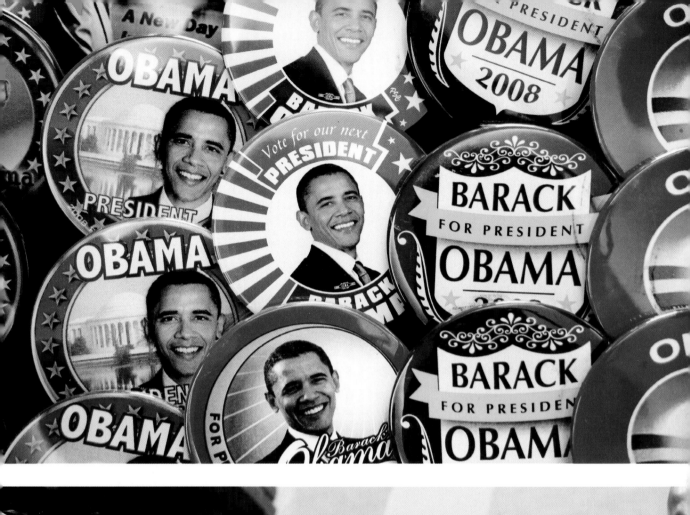

CHANGE
WE CAN
BELIEVE IN
BarackObama.com
PAID FOR BY OBAMA FOR AMERICA
BARACK OBAMA
A New
Hope
EXCLUSIVE
Inside his
people-powered
revolution
ENDORSEMENT
The candidate and
the call of history
HILLARY'S
LAST STAND
THE BLACK
CROWES
Back, better and

Supporters gather for a rally at the Xcel Energy Center in St. Paul, Minnesota, on the night Obama clinches the nomination by winning the Montana primary and securing enough pledges of support from the party's "superdelegates." In declaring that he will become the Democratic nominee, Obama tells the crowd: "AT THIS DEFINING MOMENT FOR OUR NATION, we should be proud that our party put forth one of the most talented, qualified fields of individuals ever to run for this office. I have not just competed with them as rivals, I have learned from them as friends, as public servants, and as patriots who love America and are willing to work tirelessly to make this country better."

Obama boards his campaign plane in San Antonio, Texas, on the day of the Texas primary, March 4, 2008.

Opposite: Michelle Obama attends a fund-raiser for her husband at designer Calvin Klein's home in New York, June 17, 2008. Michelle proved to be a poised, straight-talking asset for Obama—and also a lightning rod for Republican critics, who portrayed her as angry and unpatriotic. Even the New Yorker, not exactly a GOP organ, clumsily satirized her as a gun-wielding militant. Obama let political opponents know that, while he was fair game, he would not tolerate attacks on his wife. As for her fashion sense, this Ivy League graduate–turned corporate lawyer–turned Chicago hospital executive cohosted The View in a black-and-white leaf-print dress by Donna Ricco. Priced at $148 at the White House/Black Market boutiques, the dress was quickly gobbled up by women everywhere who wanted to dress like Michelle.

Obama supporters rally for their man outside the Kodak Theater in Hollywood, California, site of the first one-on-one debate between Clinton and Obama, January 31, 2008. Both candidates paused from their increasingly contentious battle to pay homage to each other and to the Democrats' history-making season.

———————————

Opposite top: Barack Obama embarks upon a four-city whistle-stop tour of Pennsylvania, riding on a train between Philadelphia and Harrisburg.

———————————

Opposite bottom: Supporters wave as Obama's train rumbles by during the whistle-stop tour.

Tears stream down a young girl's face as she listens to Obama kick off the general election campaign at a rally at the Nissan Pavilion in Bristow, Virginia, June 5, 2008.

———————————————

Opposite: Obama addresses a town-hall meeting at a high school in Bristol, Virginia, June 5, 2008.

Above: Obama signs an autograph for Kaitlyn Messersmith, 6, of Rapid City, South Dakota, while her family dines at the Firehouse Brewing Company.

————————————

Right: Here, Kaitlyn's autograph is displayed for a photographer.

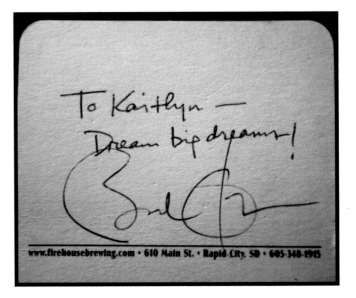

To Kaitlyn —
Dream big dreams!

www.firehousebrewing.com • 610 Main St. • Rapid City, SD • 605-348-1915

The amateur hula dance troupe, the Obama Girls, shout

"YES WE CAN!" during a rally to support

Obama, in Japan's city of Obama in the Fukui prefecture,

May 21, 2008. Obama, the candidate, has been a hit in many

parts of the world, borne out by the enthusiastic reception

he received during a trip to the Middle East and Europe in

July 2008.

Obama waves after speaking at the 2008 American Israel Public Affairs Committee (AIPAC) Policy Conference at the Washington Convention Center in Washington, D.C., June 4, 2008. Throughout the campaign, Obama met with Jewish groups, large and small, in an effort to assuage concerns about where he stood on the Israeli-Palestinian conflict and other Middle East issues. Persistent Internet falsehoods that he is a Muslim, and other rumors, dogged the campaign and created the need to take aggressive countermeasures.

Opposite: More than 20,000 people turn out for a lakeside rally in downtown Austin, Texas, February 23, 2007. Obama was at his oratorical best at big rallies, but criticism from opponents that his eloquence was not matched by substance made the campaign wary of doing too many of them.

Opposite top: The Obama campaign office in Vincennes, Indiana, was vandalized at 2 A.M. on the eve of that state's primary, according to police. A large plate-glass window was smashed, an American flag was stolen, and hate messages were spray-painted on some windows. The messages included references to Obama's controversial former pastor, the Reverand Jeremiah A. Wright, Jr., and to the militant Islamic group Hamas. This photo was taken and provided by Ray McCormick, a farmer and Obama volunteer whom police alerted to the vandalism shortly after it happened. McCormick wanted to notify the media of the incident but was was told by an Obama representative in Vincennes that top campaign officials didn't want to make a big deal of the crime. He took the photos anyway and shared them with selected news outlets. "The pictures represent what we are breaking through and overcoming," McCormick told the *Washington Post.* The Obama campaign struggled with how to deal with the blatant racism encountered by some staff, volunteers, and surrogates for the candidate. Hillary Clinton squeaked out a razor-thin victory over Obama in the May 6 Indiana primary on the same night Obama walloped her in North Carolina.

Opposite bottom: An Obama supporter pastes up posters outside the Rec-reational Sports Center at the University of Texas at Austin hours before the debate on February 21, 2008. The poster, now in wide circulation, is the creation of Shepard Fairey, an influential Los Angeles street artist and graphic designer.

Obama on his campaign plane holding forth with the media. The Obama campaign was known for its discipline, which included limited and tightly controlled opportunities for journalists to interact with the candidate.

———————————

Opposite: A crowd gathers near the state capitol for a Martin Luther King holiday rally in Columbia, South Carolina, January 21, 2008. Barack Obama, Hillary Clinton, and John Edwards all took part in the event before heading to Myrtle Beach that evening for one of the feistiest debates of the campaign.

Obama at a town hall with veterans in San Antonio, Texas, on March 3, 2008. Obama is wearing a bracelet bearing the name of Sgt. Ryan David Jopek, killed in Iraq on August 2, 2006. Early on in the campaign, Obama tried to draw a contrast with his opponents as the only major candidate who had opposed the Iraq war from the outset.

Michelle Obama looks on as Obama gives his Super Tuesday

election night speech in Chicago.

Obama and his wife, Michelle, appearing at an outdoor postelection party in San Antonio on the night of the Texas primary.

Obama holds a rally at the Kentucky International Convention Center in Louisville, May 12, 2008. Obama didn't campaign much in Kentucky prior to their primary and fared poorly, as expected, losing to Clinton by more than a 2–1 margin. Noting that Obama was under fire for his inability to make his case with working-class white voters in states such as Ohio, Pennsylvania, and West Virginia, some Democrats thought it was a mistake for him not to campaign more aggressively in Kentucky, given he was likely to be the nominee. Clinton tried to hammer at this Obama weakness as a justification to nominate her, ultimately to no avail. In Kentucky, exit polls showed Clinton winning 72 percent of white voters, compared with Obama's 23 percent; and Clinton winning 56 percent of all voters without college degrees, compared with Obama's 40 percent.

Obama even carries his own pizzas. The candidate makes an unscheduled stop at George's Pizza & Steakhouse in Fairfield, Iowa, December 9, 2007. Pizza is traditionally the number one campaign food choice for staff and volunteers.

———————————————

Opposite top: Obama comes face-to-face with Hayley Mitchell, a high-school junior in Providence, Rhode Island, who was overwhelmed meeting the candidate in person.

———————————————

Opposite bottom: Obama meets Tyrone Seay and his 15-year-old son, Elijah, after a July 3, 2007, speech in Keokuk, Iowa.

Michelle Obama with daughter Sasha (7) and the candidate with daughter Malia (10) at the Fourth of July celebrations in Butte, Montana. They attend a parade (along with Obama's sister, Maya Soetoro-Ng, and her husband, Konrad, and their daughter, Suhalia). Later, they attend a picnic at the Montana Mining Museum, where Obama speaks to the crowd, cooks hamburgers, and does an interview with *People* correspondent Sandra Sobieraj Westfall.

Obama bathed in light as he waits to speak in Aberdeen, South Dakota, May 31, 2008.

————————————————

Opposite: Obama at a rally in Washington, D.C., September 18, 2007. Behind him, D.C. mayor Adrian Fenty applauds.

Obama watches a video question during the CNN/YouTube debate at
the Citadel in Charleston, South Carolina, July 23, 2007.

Opposite: A familiar ritual: the post-debate autograph and picture-
taking session. Obama wipes sweat from his brow following a Democratic debate at Howard University in Washington, D.C., June 29, 2007.
The debate was orchestrated by commentator Tavis Smiley, who would
later come under fire from African Americans for his criticisms of
Obama and resign from *The Tom Joyner Morning Show.*

Candidates always spend time working the rope lines after speeches. That is a requirement of presidential politics. No candidate saw more HANDS REACHING OUT TO TOUCH HIM during the 2008 campaign than Obama. Here he is being congratulated in St. Paul's Xcel Energy Center (St. Paul, Minnesota) on the final election-night rally of the primary season.

The Obama campaign was able to effectively use the Internet to organize young people. Some who came to this Iowa State University rally on February 11, 2007, agreed to volunteer for Obama and were brought together through Facebook.com.

Obama shakes hands during a Broward County campaign rally at the BankAtlantic Center in Sunrise, Florida, May 23, 2008. Students, teachers, and other locals clamored to get handshakes and autographs from Obama after his speech.

Seven months before announcing his presidential campaign, Obama speaks to a crowd of supporters in a New Orleans church. Led by former North Carolina senator John Edwards, Democratic candidates highlighted the response to Hurricane Katrina as a failure in leadership by the Republican administration.

———————————————

Opposite: Obama holds a town-hall meeting at the Aberdeen Civic Arena in Aberdeen, South Dakota, May 31, 2008.

———————————————

Overleaf: This fist bump Michelle initiated with her husband in celebration of his clinching the Democratic nomination became the subject of rampant, misguided commentary. One Fox News anchor called it a "terrorist fist jab." Huh? As almost everyone with even a C average in hipness knows, that kind of "pound" or "dap" is as American as the iPod—and with greater longevity. Folks have been fist-bumping for years on basketball courts, at corporate water coolers, in barbershops, and at country clubs.

Above: The crowd of 75,000 at Waterfront Park in Portland, Oregon, on May 18, 2008, seemed to keep flowing and winding and spilling over as far as the eye could see. This aerial photograph gives some sense of the magnitude of that event.

Overleaf: Obama talks on the phone with his family during a campaign

bus trip, near Sioux City, Iowa, December 18, 2007.

A young supporter looks on as Obama speaks to a crowd during a rally at Waterfront

Park in Portland, Oregon, May 2008.

After conceding defeat in the New Hampshire primary, Obama and wife, Michelle, wave

to the crowd during a rally at Nashua South High School in Nashua, New Hampshire.

Obama posing for pictures in front of a Tulane University basketball mural.

Opposite: Basketball was a favorite campaign exercise and release for Obama, who played on his high-school team in Hawaii. During the campaign, he played pickup games with military men, reporters, and members of the North Carolina Tar Heels. He also shot games of P-I-G with teenagers. Here, he is in a 3-on-3 game in Kokomo, Indiana, on April 25, 2008. One of his constant b-ball partners is aide Reggie Love (not seen), who played both football and basketball for Duke University.

Obama appears with Massachusetts senator JOHN KERRY, the 2004 Democratic nominee, during a rally at the College of Charleston on January 10, 2008. Kerry was among a long list of highly sought after public officials who endorsed Obama at critical moments during the campaign. That said, even with the backing of Kerry, Senator Ted Kennedy, and Governor Deval Patrick, Obama still couldn't carry Massachusetts.

Obama greets former president Bill Clinton on March 4, 2007, after a reenactment of the 1965 march from Selma to Montgomery. Relations between OBAMA AND CLINTON would grow much chillier than this photo conveys. Clinton became an aggressive surrogate on behalf of his wife, going after Obama when others were reluctant to, a strategy that ultimately backfired. Several of his comments drew an angry backlash from African Americans, who had long supported him. Among those comments: Clinton called Obama's opposition to the Iraq war "a fairy tale" and seemed to dismiss and racialize Obama's overwhelming victory in South Carolina by saying Jesse Jackson won that state too. House Majority Whip James Clyburn (D-SC), the highest-ranking African American in Congress, was so incensed by Clinton's campaign tactics that he pointedly told the ex-prez to "chill out."

(Left to right) Hillary Clinton, Barack Obama, Bill Richardson, and
John Edwards together after a televised debate at Saint Anselm College in Manchester, New Hampshire, January 5, 2008.

———————————————

Opposite: Obama at a rally at Washington Square Park in New York
City, September 27, 2007.

No endorsement was bigger this campaign season than

SENATOR TED KENNEDY'S. Here,

Obama is seen with Kennedy backstage before a rally to unveil

the endorsement at American University in Washington, D.C.

Also backstage is Caroline Kennedy Schlossberg, daughter

of the late president John F. Kennedy. She also endorsed

Obama and later was named to the committee overseeing

his search for a vice-presidential running mate. Most of the

Kennedy clan, though not all, fell in line behind Obama and

campaigned tirelessly for the senator. Senator Kennedy had

been courted heavily by both Obama and Clinton, and was

said to be disappointed in some of the negative campaign

tactics employed by the Clintons.

Left: Barack Obama rallies New York at Washington Square Park.

———————

Below: Obama flashes a big smile as he greets supporters on March 18, 2007, after speaking before an enthusiastic Denver crowd that paid $100 each for a chance to hear what one of the front-running Democratic candidates had to say.

Above: Obama hugs a resident of Albia, Iowa, during an unplanned campaign stop on November 8, 2007.

————————

Right: Barack Obama at Time Warner's Conversations on the Circle in New York.

Barack Obama and Hillary Clinton come separately to Selma, Alabama, to commemorate the civil rights movement and march across the EDMUND PETTUS BRIDGE, where civil rights activists were badly beaten by police during an attempted march in 1965. One of those beaten was Rep. John Lewis (D-GA), the former Student Nonviolent Coordinating Committee (SNCC) leader who was aggressively courted by both candidates. Lewis, after much deliberation, endorsed Clinton but later switched to Obama after the tide in the campaign shifted. Lewis came under fire in Atlanta after Obama carried his congressional district overwhelmingly on Super Tuesday. Like many black politicians who supported Clinton this year, Lewis found himself harassed and threatened with reprisals. However, despite challenges to his congressional seat, Lewis had no difficulty defeating his opponents.

Senator Chris Dodd of Connecticut and Obama react to audience members after the Iowa Brown & Black Forum in Des Moines, December 1, 2007. Dodd was one of the early dropouts in the Democratic race, and the first to endorse Obama after abandoning his own bid.

————————————

Opposite top: Former Dallas Cowboys running back Emmitt Smith warms up the crowd at an Obama rally at Reunion Arena in Dallas, February 20, 2008.

————————————

Opposite bottom: Apparently with visions of a "dream ticket," one person holds up pictures of Clinton *and* Obama during a Clinton campaign event at the University of Miami, May 22, 2008.

Obama campaign communications director Robert Gibbs (left) and chief strategist David Axelrod (right) talk to reporters on the campaign plane en route to a rally, June 3, 2008.

Opposite: Obama strides toward the stage for a rally at Nissan Pavilion in Bristow, Virginia, June 5, 2008.

Obama peers through a kaleidoscope while shopping for gifts for his wife and daughters at Prairie Edge in the downtown shopping district of Rapid City, South Dakota.

───────────────

Opposite top: Ariel Ritchin, a citizen outreach canvasser for Grassroots Campaigns, raises funds and registers volunteers for the Democratic National Committee at 12th Street and University Place in downtown Manhattan.

───────────────

Opposite bottom: Obama, holding youngest daughter, Sasha, during a 2007 campaign appearance in New Hampshire.

Obama fund-raising reception at a Park Avenue apartment in New York, March 27, 2008. Here, Margarett Cooper and Lizzy Cooper Davis meet Barack Obama up close.

———————————————

Opposite: Obama cleans a table in the home of John Thornton while working with Pauline Beck (not pictured) during the Walk a Day in My Shoes program in Oakland, California. Obama spent the morning of August 8, 2007, with Beck, a home health-care worker, first meeting her at her home in Alameda and then going to her job site, where she cares for Thornton. The program is part of an effort by a local union to have presidential candidates walk in voters' shoes for a day.

Father Michael Pfleger (left) and the Reverend Jesse Jackson (right) attend an anti-gun rally outside the manufacturing facilities of D. S. Arms in Barrington, Illinois, August 28, 2007. Both Pfleger and Jackson, Obama supporters, would become problems for the candidate. Jackson challenged Obama's emphasis in some speeches on promoting faith-based social services and personal responsibility. "The message to black America has to have broader application so that it doesn't appear to be limited in scope," Jackson said in an interview. Pfleger was admonished by the Obama campaign and the Catholic Church for a sermon in which he promised to expose "white entitlement and supremacy wherever it raises its head." He also mocked Hillary Clinton as someone crying over "a black man stealing my show." Obama declared that he was "deeply disappointed" in Pfleger for his "divisive, backward-looking rhetoric." Pfleger's guest sermon, delivered at Trinity United Church of Christ in Chicago, appeared to be the last straw in what had become for Obama an uneasy relationship with his home church. On May 31, 2008, not long after Pfleger's sermon hit YouTube, Obama and Michelle announced they had left Trinity.

The Reverend Jeremiah A. Wright, Jr., speaks at the NAACP's 53rd Annual Fight for Freedom Fund Dinner at Cobo Hall in Detroit, Michigan, April 27, 2008. No one caused Obama more heartache this campaign season than Wright, his longtime pastor who married him and baptized his children. A series of controversial remarks, caught in snippets and often distorted on YouTube, ultimately led Obama to sever ties with Wright. The final trigger was Wright's defiant appearance at the National Press Club in Washington on April 28, 2008. In resigning from Trinity, the Obamas noted the sadness of their decision. But in their letter to the Reverend Otis Moss III, the head pastor, the couple also noted how relations "have been strained by the divisive statements of Reverend Wright, which sharply conflict with our own views."

Fund-raiser for Obama in Princeton, New Jersey, at the home
of Paula and Noel Gordon. (Left to right) Jeff Palmer, Obama,
Deborah Brittain, and Willard Brittain.

Opposite: Obama delivers the commencement address at
Wesleyan University in Middletown, Connecticut, May 25,
2008. He stepped in for Senator Edward M. Kennedy, who was
diagnosed the same week with a cancerous brain tumor.

So what else is new? Standing in long lines to get into a Barack Obama event is customary, whether it be a rally at a local high school or a swank fund-raiser. In Washington, D.C., the line is long outside the Avenue nightclub. But patrons are patient as they wait to mix and mingle at a campaign fund-raising party.

———————————

Opposite: Oprah Winfrey lends her prestige to Obama, addressing a campaign rally at the Verizon Wireless Arena in Manchester, New Hampshire, December 9, 2007. Winfrey is not known to get involved in electoral politics, so this was a real leap for her. Though she smoothly handles the duties of talk-show host, she acknowledged she was nervous on the campaign stage.

The May 19, 2008, cover of *Time* magazine features a portrait of a smiling Obama accompanied by the caption "And the Winner Is . . . (Really, we're pretty sure this time)." The cover infuriated Clintonites, who cited it as more evidence of the drumbeat by the media establishment and Democratic leaders to ease their candidate out of the race.

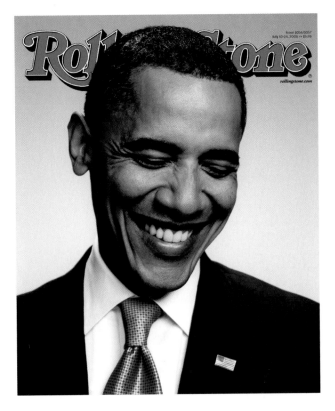

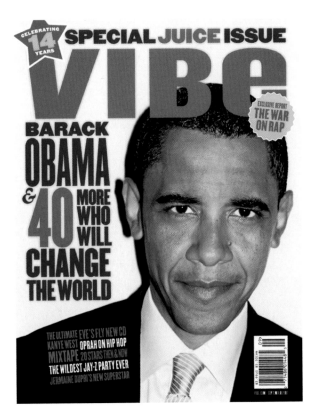

SPECIAL JUICE ISSUE

VIBE

CELEBRATING 14 YEARS

EXCLUSIVE REPORT
THE WAR ON RAP

BARACK
OBAMA
& 40 MORE
WHO
WILL
CHANGE
THE WORLD

THE ULTIMATE EVE'S FLY NEW CD
KANYE WEST OPRAH ON HIP HOP
MIXTAPE 20 STARS THEN & NOW
THE WILDEST JAY-Z PARTY EVER
JERMAINE DUPRI'S NEW SUPERSTAR

BLACK
ENTERPRISE

Bargain Stocks For 2008

YOUR ULTIMATE SOURCE FOR WEALTH CREATION

January 2008

The Next
Generation
Of Young, Rich
Entrepreneurs

Develop Your
Estate Plan
The Right Way

Why
Barack
Obama
Should Be
President

The Onion Magazine

OCTOBER 29, 2006

Does Barack Obama Have
What It Takes To Become
The Lowest-Paid President
In American History?

By Catherine Sorren

Obama senior campaign spokeswoman Linda Douglass (center) reviews the news of the day with Obama and his wife, Michelle, in a private room after a speech in Columbus, Ohio, June 13, 2008. Douglass left ABC News to join the campaign and travel with the candidate, adding media experience to the communications operation.

Opposite: Obama during a town-hall-style meeting at Kennedy High School in Cedar Rapids, Iowa.

For more than thirty years, Elise Martin served as poll manager in Columbia, South Carolina. She had thought of retiring from that job at the end of 2007. However, when she heard Obama was running, and that her granddaughter was working in the campaign, she decided to stay on through the primary, held on January 26, 2008. On primary day, Obama dropped by the polling place she managed at Benedict College. A friend came over to get her. As the picture was being taken, she told Obama that she had originally planned to retire from poll work but decided to hang in there for one more campaign. "I AM A 93-YEAR-OLD WOMAN WORKING THE POLLS BECAUSE YOU ARE RUNNING," Martin told Obama. "Never give up because I know you can win."

A fan snaps a photo of Obama while he signs autographs at a town hall with veterans in San Antonio, Texas.

Opposite top: Chris Hughes, 24, a founder of Facebook, left the company to develop Senator Barack Obama's Web presence.

Opposite bottom: Barack Obama with some campaign essentials: the Secret Service, traveling aides, and his BlackBerry.

Obama and Clinton talk on the plane en route to their Unity rally in Unity, New Hampshire, June 27, 2008. After a bruising battle, questions of how to unify the party remained. Some of Clinton's supporters were having difficulty accepting Obama as the presumptive nominee. Other issues lingered: Would the Obama campaign incorporate into its operations top Clinton staffers? (Yes, a few, including Clinton's chief speech writer and her onetime campaign manager Patti Solis Doyle.) What role would Clinton play at the Democratic National Convention and in the fall campaign? (She would give a major address on the convention's second night and pledge to campaign tirelessly.) And, most significant, would Obama choose Clinton as his running mate? (No.)

Obama draws a small crowd on a block in West Philadelphia on the day of the Pennsylvania primary, April 22, 2008.

————————————

Opposite: Obama shaking hands in New Hampshire.

————————————

Overleaf: Obama holds a baby for the classic American political photo op in Westerville, Ohio, March 2, 2008.

At a campaign event in Philadelphia in May 2007.

Opposite: Obama gives keynote speech and receives an honorary Doctor of Laws degree at Howard University's 140th opening convocation in September 2007. Flanking Obama are Southeastern University president, Dr. Charlene Drew Jarvis (left), and Howard's president, H. Patrick Swygert (right).

Obama answers a question before the National Association of Latino Elected and Appointed Officials (NALEO). Both Obama and McCain addressed the group. Both have assiduously courted Latino voters. Polls have indicated Obama has the edge over McCain with Latinos, despite Obama's problems making inroads during the Democratic primaries because of the strong loyalty the Clintons commanded.

Obama stands with his powerhouse Massachusetts support group, which includes

at least two people mentioned as possible cabinet members in an Obama admin-

istration: John Kerry as secretary of state? Deval Patrick as attorney general?

Speaker of the House Nancy Pelosi (right) and Democratic National Committee chairman Howard Dean (left) listen during a news conference at DNC headquarters in Washington, D.C., June 10, 2008. Some Democrats worried that the protracted presidential campaign fight slowed efforts to establish a coordinated Democratic fall campaign that would extend down the ballot from the top of the ticket. Pelosi and Dean, though publicly neutral, came under fire from some Clinton supporters who believed the two party leaders were partial to Obama and had tried to hasten Clinton's departure from the race.

Opposite: Chelsea Clinton and her father, former president Bill Clinton, look on as Senator Hillary Rodham Clinton greets supporters who packed the National Building Museum in Washington, D.C. The suspension of her campaign brought together close friends and many luminaries from the Clinton White House years, as well as feminist pioneers such as Gloria Steinem.

Clinton throws her support behind Obama at an EMOTIONAL RALLY at the National Building Museum in Washington, D.C., June 7, 2008. Clinton staff and volunteers traveled from across the country to say farewell to their candidate, who fell just short of making history herself. Clinton promised to do everything she could to send her rival to the White House.

Opposite: Michelle, Malia, Sasha, and the Illinois senator take the stage during a rally near the Iowa state capitol building in Des Moines, Iowa, May 20, 2008.

————————

Above: Obama looks to the crowd after delivering a speech in Plainfield, Indiana, March 15, 2008. As usual, the cell phone photographers are always in abundance.

————————

Right: Obama holds a copy of his book *The Audacity of Hope* after speaking at a rally at George Mason University in Fairfax, Virginia.

Kenya's newspapers are displayed in the streets of Nairobi with headlines claiming Obama as a native son and trumpeting his achievement in securing the Democratic nomination. Obama has maintained ties to family members in Kenya, following a 1987 pilgrimage to the country to untangle the mystery of his father and discover his roots.

Opposite: Obama and former vice president Al Gore appear onstage together after Gore publicly endorsed him at a rally at Joe Louis Arena, in Detroit, Michigan, June 16, 2008. After Gore won an Oscar and the Nobel Peace Prize for his environmental work, some Democrats thought he might be a better candidate this time around than he was in 2000. But Gore chose to sit this one out.

Democratic presidential nominee Senator Barack Obama
with his vice presidential nominee, Senator Joe Biden, after
Biden addressed the 2008
Democratic National Convention in Denver.

It began on a frigid, 7-degree

morning in Springfield, Illinois, in the shadow of the Old State Capitol, where in 1858 Abraham Lincoln delivered his famous House Divided speech against slavery. Packed into every square foot of the grounds, thousands of the brave and faithful scrunched together to keep warm as they waited for another tall, thin lawyer—this one without a beard—to begin his own march toward history. At just after 10:00 A.M. on February 10, 2007, Barack Obama bopped onto the stage in a black overcoat and scarf, hatless and gloveless, a forty-five-year-old political insurgent on a seemingly impossible journey. Accompanied by his wife, Michelle, and young daughters, Sasha and Malia, he surveyed the crowd, clapped his hands, and honored God for the occasion.

"I know it's a little chilly, but I'm fired up!"

Launching his campaign for president, Obama said: "I recognize there is a certain presumptuousness—a certain audacity—to this announcement. I know I haven't spent a lot of time learning the ways of Washington. But I've been there long enough to know that the ways of Washington must change."

Change—coupled with hope—would become Obama's mantra during an eighteen-month odyssey that took him from that winter morning in Springfield to the Democratic nomination, a feat that defied conventional wisdom and cemented his place in American political lore. He had become what many had only dreamed about and others could never imagine seeing in their lifetimes: the first African American presidential nominee of a major party, one November victory away from the Oval Office.

Beyond the symbolism and emotion of this achievement, in pure political terms Obama's triumph was astonishing. He rewrote the presidential campaign playbook, using the modern tools of technology to mobilize hundreds of thousands of volunteers across the country, turn out his voters, and shatter fund-raising records. By the summer of 2008, Obama had raised nearly $340 million, more than any presidential candidate ever. Many of the contributions were small amounts from first-time, online donors.

Using the model of social networking sites—he even lured to his team one of Facebook's founders—Obama empowered supporters in local communities to host house parties, stay in touch with one another, and create their own affiliated campaign groups through My.BarackObama.com. To more aggressively combat rampant Internet rumors and falsehoods about his religion, heritage, and patriotism, Obama constructed a separate Web site, FighttheSmears.com. This would not be a 1.0 kind of campaign. He staffed his field operations with energetic twenty-somethings, many of whom had never been involved in politics at any level. Obama became a new voice for this generation, hip enough to have Jay-Z on his iPod and to inspire a music video by Will.i.am. Kids who didn't even believe in student government—much less the federal government—led Obama's rally chants: "Yes We Can! Yes We Can!" And the rallies spilled out into the streets and parks like concerts.

Winning the nomination wasn't easy. Obama had to defeat the First Couple of the Democratic Party, Hillary and Bill Clinton, who often seemed to run as a tandem. Bill Clinton is the most successful Democrat of the modern era, the only two-term president the party can claim since Franklin D. Roosevelt. As her husband's partner in the White House and now the junior senator from New York, Hillary Clinton began the 2008 presidential campaign with a formidable organization and fund-raising network, high name recognition, and her own history-making appeal to become America's first female president. She quickly emerged as the odds-on favorite and candidate of the party establishment. Early polls gave her a twenty- to thirty-point lead over Obama, her closest rival in a crowded field of competitors.

But as in that old children's fable, Obama was the tortoise whom the hare underestimated. It was as if the political gods had whispered to him: This is your time. A soaring keynote speech at the 2004 Democratic National Convention had transformed this unknown state senator into a national sensation. A 2006 bestseller, *The Audacity of Hope*, catapulted him further into the stratosphere. He became the hottest draw on the Democratic fund-raising circuit—the hottest draw on any circuit. Crowds overflowed wherever he appeared publicly.

Still, it was easy to understand why Obama mentioned a "certain audacity" when announcing his

presidential candidacy: He had been a United States senator for just twenty-five months, a state senator prior to that for not even seven years. The rest of his résumé read like this: Chicago community organizer, graduate of Harvard Law School, civil rights attorney, University of Chicago law school instructor, failed congressional candidate, author. All in a twenty-year period. And now this young man wanted to be leader of the free world? Some said he was too green, too cocky. The Clintons thought he was all glib and glitz, more show than substance—but with a bright future. If only he would wait his turn.

Former Dallas mayor Ron Kirk remembers talking to Obama during the period in late 2006 when he was mulling a presidential run. Kirk himself was among the party's bright African American political stars, a former United States Senate nominee who had run one of the nation's ten largest cities. "I could not give him a compelling reason why he should wait,"

Kirk recalled. "The type of appeal he has right now doesn't come around often. Political capital has to be spent in the marketplace at the right time."

And then Kirk paused. Barack Obama reminded him of Tiger Woods. "I think there is something really magical about this brother."

*   *   *

What does magic look like?

The pictures collected in this volume show Obama's effortlessness, his cool, his contemplative side, his solemn side, his playful side. His disappointment and his joy. We see him onstage, jacketless, in a white dress shirt, the sleeves rolled up to just below the elbows (his favorite campaign uniform), exhorting, challenging, trying to lift up and not let down. It's hard to miss his campaign slogan, always somewhere on somebody's sign in the background: Change We Can Believe In! The son of

a white Kansas mother who traveled widely and a black Kenyan father who deserted him, Obama was raised in part by his white grandparents. He grew up in Hawaii and Indonesia. Not in Gary or Detroit. Not two blocks from the riots. But the "brother" in him is never far from observation—whether in his walk, his dap, his juke to the hoop, or in the familiar way he connects with a small black crowd on a West Philly street corner. A brother, but a brother whose countenance conveys: without limitations. Biracial, citizen of the world. Part of the marvel of photography is that it freezes moments, allowing us to study them, ponder their meaning, return to them for new insights. What was Obama thinking about when *Washington Post* photographer Jahi Chikwendiu caught him ascending the ramp to his

campaign plane on the day of the Pennsylvania primary, a lone silhouetted figure, head slightly bowed, bag slung over his right shoulder, a jet taking flight in the distance? Where would we be without the photographer marching us to images we'd otherwise never notice? Obama alone on his cell phone in some colorless concrete holding room in Omaha. Obama struggling to tuck a cloth napkin inside the collar of his starched shirt, not wanting to risk soiling his campaign uniform as he prepared to take a private meal. At a veterans' event in San Antonio, *Post* photographer Linda Davidson zoomed in on Obama's hands, just his hands, which were clasped as if in prayer. How often do we get to take the measure of a candidate's hands, to be brought so close we can see veins and wrinkles and knuckles and short, uneven fingernails, close enough to make a judgment about what those hands say? Obama seemed different from the outset, not so much because of his pretty words and the cadence with which he delivered them. That was the critics' rap on him, right? *Just words.* No, he seemed different because of the effect he had on others—the miles they were willing to drive to see him, the lines they were willing to stand in to hear him, the jobs they were willing to leave to work for him, the reactions they had when they met him. Take Davidson's shot of high-school junior Hayley Mitchell, her hands flapping with excitement, her mouth open in an Oh-My-Gosh! shriek upon coming face-to-face with Obama at a Providence rally. It was like she had just met Usher.

When Obama won the Iowa caucuses, January 3, 2008, winning the presidency for him suddenly became real. "If I had lost Iowa," he would later tell volunteers and staffers, "it would have been over."

The pictures from that night show the beaming face of a candidate whose audacity had been rewarded. His campaign's brain trust, amid the doubts of some fund-raisers, had spent heavily and organized furiously in this tiny state, treating Iowa like it was their Waterloo. It marked the successful beginning of a strategy to amass delegates by winning small-state caucuses, which are essentially organizing competitions. With his wife and daughters sharing the victory stage that night in Des Moines, Obama never stopped smiling. He clutched Sasha with his right arm and waved with his left, as both girls pointed to people in the crowd and Mommy stretched her arms out wide as if to embrace the good feeling.

"You know, they said this day would never come," Obama began, thanking Iowans. "They said our

Family victory night in Iowa: Obama with daughter Sasha in one arm; daughter Malia pointing to someone in the crowd; Michelle soaking up the scene as her husband racks up his first win.

sights were set too high. They said this country was too divided, too disillusioned to ever come together around a common purpose. But on this January night, at this defining moment in history, you have done what the cynics said we couldn't do."

* * *

History has a way of leading us to undiscovered treasure.

Buried in the bowels of the past is the extraordinary story of John Mercer Langston, one of the most accomplished Americans of the nineteenth century, but largely forgotten. He was Barack Obama before Barack Obama. Elected first to local office in Ohio in 1855 and later serving as Virginia's first black congressman, Langston was one of the early African American political pioneers. Breaking down the walls to elective office, he gave doubtful, hateful white Americans a new view of black leadership. A prominent abolitionist and founder of what would become the Howard University School of Law, Langston was both a close associate and sometime rival of Frederick Douglass. Douglass, of course, was the better known of the two; statesmanlike, popular, accessible. He could have been elected president himself if the times had allowed. But Langston, some argue, might have been the better choice.

Few black men of that period had a broader range of achievement and abilities: A graduate of Oberlin College, Langston had served as educational inspector for the Freedmen's Bureau, had been the U.S. minister to Haiti, and was perhaps the most sought-after black surrogate of the Republican Party.

What is striking is how much Obama has in common with Langston. Like Obama, Langston was of mixed-race parentage (his father a white slave-owner, his mother an ex-slave and bondswoman). Like Obama, Langston was tall, wiry, light-skinned, an expert in constitutional law, and a gifted orator. Both were drawn to community organizing (Langston went around Ohio organizing schools).

Like Obama, Langston knew how to skillfully maneuver in both the black and white worlds and sought to bridge the racial divide after the Civil War.

"Langston was certainly capable of being president in the nineteenth century," observed historian William Cheek, coauthor of a two-volume biography of Langston.

But the country wasn't ready.

History finds ways to reward patience. Many African American politicians had the desire to become president, and the promise. But there was sometimes not the courage to run, the daring to risk one's safe position.

Jesse Jackson's decision to run for president in 1984 seemed to many at the time like a brazen act of symbolism and ego. Now it seems profound. Jackson's 1984 campaign grew out of a series of private meetings among prominent black political and civil rights figures who wondered: Is now the time for an African American to mount a serious bid for the presidency? And if so, who? For years, black elected officials had struggled with these questions. In 1972, New York congresswoman Shirley Chisholm became the first African American of stature to launch a presidential campaign, running under the slogan Unbought and Unbossed. Her candidacy turned into a feminist cause célèbre, and she was awarded a coveted speaking slot at the Democratic National Convention. That in itself was progress, according to several veteran black politicians, who recalled earlier conventions when they were reduced to slipping notes into the trailers of major candidates, hoping to get a meeting.

Fast-forward to 1983. Many black leaders were encouraged by Harold Washington's election as Chicago's first black mayor and increasingly worried about the impact on black communities of Ronald Reagan's presidency. Yet, none of the big-name black elected officials—notably Andrew Young, then the Atlanta mayor—would take the plunge and try out for the Oval Office. Some didn't want to jeopardize their standing with the eventual Democratic nominee. Others offered assorted explanations, all of which amounted to fear or practicality or the bottom line: A black candidate can't win. That Jackson raised his hand when no one else would was a feat by itself. His is the biggest shoulder Obama stands on. By winning five Democratic primaries and caucuses, Jackson lapped expectations and laid the groundwork for a more robust second campaign. In 1988, Jackson won eleven primaries and caucuses, doubled his total votes to nearly seven million, and finished as runner-up to Democratic nominee Michael Dukakis.

More significant, his campaigns opened up the Democratic Party infrastructure to new field-workers, campaign strategists, and volunteers who had never participated in electoral politics—much like Obama is doing in 2008, in a different way. It was also Jackson who pushed through a change in party rules that proved crucial to Obama's success. Because delegates are now awarded proportionally in Democratic primaries and caucuses, instead of the previous winner-take-all system, Obama was able to build a lead that Clinton could never overtake, despite her winning nine of the last fifteen contests.

When Jackson was running in 1984, Obama was a recent Columbia University graduate, still sorting out what he wanted to become. Watching Jackson debate Walter Mondale and Gary Hart on television had inspired him, Obama once told the civil rights leader. Though Jackson endorsed Obama early, he was not asked to campaign for him, a slight that wounded Jackson, whose ego is easily bruised. Later in the campaign, relations between the pioneer and the newcomer took a blow when Jackson was caught unaware on an open television microphone complaining to a fellow guest that Obama had been "talking down" to black people in some of his speeches. "I want to cut his nuts off," Jackson whispered to the guest. He later apologized to Obama, who graciously accepted it. But the episode was another reminder that Obama is now more in sync with another Jesse Jackson—Big Jesse's son Junior, the congressman from Chicago who is one of Obama's national campaign cochairmen.

Getting to this point in history has hardly been relaxing. Just imagining an African American president has taken work.

I am reminded of a conversation I had with Christopher Edley, Jr., in 2000. Edley had worked for candidates and presidents dating back to the Carter administration, and was then teaching at Harvard Law School after a tour in the Clinton White House, including serving as President Clinton's chief race adviser. Edley has this brilliant way of reducing complex subjects to their essence. I was writing a political column and asked him to speculate on the prospects of a black president by 2020, figuring that twenty years into the new millennium was distant enough to ponder the possibility as an attainable landmark.

"I'm pessimistic about that," Edley said without hesitation. "I think we will see a woman or Latino before we see an African American."

Edley's response wasn't just a nod to the booming Latino population or a reflection of some psychic instinct that Hillary Clinton, whom he had observed up close, was destined to be a serious threat. No, Edley knew that the upper ranks of elective office were "still very segregated territory," as he put it, especially the Senate and governors' mansions, which traditionally produce the most viable presidential candidacies. Even today, Obama is the nation's only African American in the Senate, and there are only two black governors: Deval Patrick of Massachusetts and David Paterson of New York. And how many Obamas are in the pipeline? Less than 4 percent of the nation's elected officials are black; and 90 percent of them serve districts where the majority of voters are nonwhite.

When I caught up with Edley at the outset of the 2008 campaign season, I reminded him of his earlier forecast, the fact that he could not even envision a black president at the turn of the century. "Wow," he said, followed by a long pause. "I hope it's evidence that I'm a lousy prognosticator, because the evidence now is there is a lot more capacity for hopefulness among the electorate than I had thought."

Historian Kenneth O'Reilly, author of *Nixon's Piano: Presidents and Racial Politics from Washington to Clinton*, says: "The number of people who are still bitter about race, who are still bitter about what happened to the South, who are still bitter about Watts, Newark, and a number of other race riots, are declining because they're passing away. What's happening is race as a force in our political structure is nowhere near as powerful as it used to be. It's still pretty strong, but it might not be strong enough to prevent Obama from winning."

Obama had to expand the hopefulness that Edley now sees and to nurture it.

He had to beat back silliness: Is Barack Obama black enough? And assuage fears: Won't someone try to kill him? And boost faith: How can a black man, even a biracial one, get elected president in a country with such an ugly legacy of slavery, segregation, and persistent racism?

"Now, I've heard that some folks aren't sure America is ready for an African American president," Obama told a black audience in Manning, South Carolina, two months before the primary there. "So let me be clear. I never would have begun this campaign if I weren't confident I could win. But you see, I am not asking anyone to take a chance on me. I am asking you to take a chance on your own aspirations."

And then Obama tried to seal the deal with an explicit racial appeal, rare for him.

"Imagine a president who was raised, like I was, by a single mom who had to work and go to school and raise her kids and accept food stamps for a while. Imagine a president who could go into Holly Court Apartments here in Manning or Scott's Branch High School in Summerton and give the young men and women there someone to look up to."

The impact of Obama's candidacy on aspirations can't be overstated. Among the most powerful images of this campaign are the pictures of ordinary people,

especially older African Americans, quietly crying. There is such a photo in this book, of a Texas woman in prayerful pose, eyes closed, tears streaming down her face at an Obama rally in Dallas.

Aspirations?

Think about Anthony Simonovich. He had never worked in a campaign before when he walked into Obama headquarters in Scranton, Pennsylvania. He had been downtown looking for work, mall work, any work. He was twenty-seven, had no college degree, and was something of a wanderer. As the product of an interracial union, he related to Obama. He could speak street and speak Shakespeare. He listened to Pink Floyd and Jay-Z. "I actually think biracial people are their own group: ZebraHead Posse."

Simonovich started out as a volunteer registering voters. Soon he was put in charge of calling voters, urging them to the polls. He was added to the payroll and given a title: phone bank director. He didn't even own a cell phone. But he had experience as a telemar-

keter, cared about the environment, and had quirky ideas that the campaign folks loved. And tattoos galore, like "havoc" and "peace" on opposite forearms. When Obama came to Scranton, Simonovich helped the Secret Service secure the area behind the community center where the candidate was to speak. The agents were grateful. Almost overnight, Simonovich had taken on a new identity. A promising romance developed. And the long campaign days? Not a problem. Four hours of sleep a night, every night, only seemed to energize him.

"We're like a family here," he said. "Everybody's last name is Obama."

By the time the Pennsylvania primary campaign had ended, Simonovich had gained new confidence in his own possibilities.

"I'm motivated," he said. "It's exciting to be a part of something this big. I'll never forget it. I'll probably get a tattoo to help me remember it."

Over time, not only had Obama buoyed the confidence of campaign workers, but nearly all those associated with him began to believe he would be the next president. They developed a swagger that many had never seen before on behalf of a black candidate.

During an American Film Institute symposium in Silver Spring, Maryland, the filmmaker Spike Lee cut off a questioner who asked how movies and culture would change if Obama were to be elected president. "There's no if," Lee corrected, before continuing. "It changes everything," he said. "It changes the world. So, it's going to be Before Barack, *B.B.*, and After Barack, *A.B.*" So certain was Lee that Obama would defeat Republican senator John McCain of Arizona, he told the audience, "I'm booking my hotel reservation now," seven months in advance of the inauguration.

Some, however, worry that the expectations being heaped on Obama are too great. Fitzgerald Barnes, the only black supervisor in Louisa County, Virginia, believes. "People's hopes are so high, and they are putting so much in him, I hope they don't expect too much—like he's our savior or something."

* * *

After Obama won Iowa, it got real interesting.

That twenty-four-point polling lead Clinton once held among black voters nationally? Forget about it. If Barack Obama could win amid the cornfields of Iowa, in a state that is 91 percent white, then maybe he could win the whole thing. Black voters started looking at him differently, euphorically. And that shift in mind-set would prove crucial. Meanwhile, the Clinton campaign seemed on the brink of self-destruction: bickering, finger-pointing. Obama jumped to a double-digit lead in New Hampshire, site of the next contest,

and the media wags started writing Clinton's obituaries. Prematurely, that is. Had Obama won the New Hampshire primary, it would have been like Buster Douglas dropping Mike Tyson to the canvas in 1990. The aura of invincibility would have been broken for keeps. But Clinton began to show her emotional side, campaigned fiercely, and found her voice, as she put it. By the time the New Hampshire results rolled in, Clinton had become the Comeback Gal. The momentum had shifted.

That night in New Hampshire, it was hard for Obama to mask his dejection. He tried, as he talked about the long march ahead, about how he always knew "our climb would be steep." But you could tell he thought he had her, and had let her slip away.

Now, it was on to South Carolina. This was the first test of black voter allegiance because of the outsize influence African Americans traditionally wield in the Democratic primary there. Both Obama and Clinton had spent considerable time organizing the state, which at times looked as if it were hosting a national black family reunion. Notables of every distinction made their way to South Carolina, from megastar Oprah to the clownish Chris Tucker, from mayors to congressmen, from black Harvard Law School alums to Delta sorority sisters. South Carolina was a war. It was where Bill Clinton first got in serious trouble with African Americans, many of whom thought he was too disparaging of Obama in his zeal to get his wife elected. This was a strange new experience for Bill, whom Toni Morrison had once labeled, to her regret, "the first black president." During a South Carolina brawl of a debate, cosponsored by the Congressional Black Caucus Institute, Obama decided to have some

Barack and Michelle Obama embrace at a rally after he was narrowly defeated in the New Hampshire primary. The loss was a tremendous disappointment for Obama, who not only had a sizable lead in New Hampshire but had control of the race coming out of the Iowa caucuses. Michelle was a mainstay during big moments in the campaign, comforting him when necessary and firing him up when necessary.

fun when asked if he believed Morrison was right. "Well," Obama began, he'd first have to "investigate Bill's dancing abilities" before he could accurately assess whether the former president "was a brother."

Not only did Obama wallop Clinton by a two-to-one margin, he won 78 percent of the black vote, according to exit polls. From that point on, the black vote was all but out of reach for Clinton. That night, many of the Obama staff celebrated at Ruth's Chris Steak House in downtown Columbia, the state capital. I ran into Obama pollster Cornell Belcher holding forth in a big booth, swigging Veuve Clicquot from the bottle. I teased him: "When are you gonna upgrade to Cristal?" "When the nomination is won," he replied. "Then we'll uncork the Cristal."

There would be no Cristal anytime soon. The Democratic primary race turned into a long, surreal slog, unlike any competition party regulars had ever witnessed. John Edwards, the Democrats' promising 2004 vice-presidential nominee, was the last major contender to drop out, after a poor showing in South Carolina. Under the Clinton camp's calculation, the race was supposed to be over on Super Tuesday, February 5, when twenty-two states held primaries and caucuses. Clinton had anticipated delivering her knockout then. But that didn't happen. She won the big states (California, New York, New Jersey). But Obama won more states (thirteen to her nine), and more delegates. During a stretch after Super Tuesday, Obama reeled off ten straight victories, and it looked like he had the thing wrapped up. It would take Clinton a month to reappear as a winner, but she came back with big triumphs in Ohio and then Pennsylvania. Obama just couldn't close the deal. As they battled on, attention turned to the all-powerful, Oz-like superdelegates, those nearly eight hundred party leaders and elected officials who were not bound by primary results and could pick the candidate of their choice. They loomed as the final deciders in this close skirmish in which neither candidate could seem to tally enough delegates to lock down the nomination. Gradually, then speedily, the supers started moving Obama's way.

While the meticulous counting of delegates was unfolding, the country often seemed to be in a debate with itself. Was it ready to elect a woman or a black man? Was sexism a bigger impediment than racism? Obama, at times, struggled with how to handle race. No episode was more torturous for him than the saga of the Reverend Jeremiah A. Wright, Jr., his Chicago pastor who was a father figure to him and had baptized his daughters. Video snippets of controversial Wright sermons ("God damn America"), widely available on YouTube, had forced Obama first to gently distance himself from Wright, then to give a major address on race, and finally to sever all ties with the minister and leave Trinity United Church of Christ altogether. It pained Obama to do it.

The irony was that Wright's body of work, and his service, was in the prophetic tradition of many other black preachers—including some we've heard of.

Harsh words for one's country, one's government? The Reverend Martin Luther King, Jr., once called the U.S. government "the greatest purveyor of violence" in the world. He also spoke of the "cultural homicide" committed against blacks in America, how their worth was devalued while white superiority was promoted. And yet he had faith in humanity, loved his country, pushed to make it better.

On the day Obama gave his carefully calibrated speech on race in Philadelphia, one of his finest moments of the campaign, Ted Shaw, a Columbia University law professor and the former head of the NAACP Legal Defense and Educational Fund, marveled at the candidate's dexterity in traversing what he called a racial tightrope.

"Senator Obama will continue to have to walk this fine line—not to be engulfed by this issue of race and on the other hand not deny his experience and identity as an African American man," Shaw said. "It shows the continued saliency of race in this country and how devilishly tricky it is for someone in his position who is trying to lead our nation and garner the support of everyone. I thank God I don't have that challenge."

On June 3, after a flood of superdelegate endorsements and a victory in the Montana primary, Obama mounted a stage in St. Paul, Minnesota, and finally claimed his prize: "Tonight, I can stand before you and say that I will be the Democratic nominee for president of the United States." It wouldn't become official until late August at the Democratic National Convention in Denver. But days later, Hillary Clinton acknowledged the inevitable and endorsed Obama.

Free now to begin his general-election campaign against McCain, Obama quickly tangled with his Senate colleague over the economy and national security. He took a trip to the Mideast and Europe, drawing two hundred thousand in Berlin and reaffirming his status as America's No. 1 rock-star politician—which McCain found hard to stomach. What to do? He ran an ad mocking Obama's celebrity persona, likening him to Paris Hilton and Britney Spears—a move that puzzled even Republicans. And race? It didn't take long for that smoldering topic to be reintroduced—this time by the McCain campaign, which accused Obama of "playing the race card." You know, that squishy, catchall phrase that is a 1990s throwback to the O. J. Simpson trial. It is the cousin of "political correctness," another charged, goofy phrase that has wormed itself into the American lexicon as the easy way to dismiss grievances without actually examining them.

What exactly is a race card? It's whatever the hurler of the charge says it is, but always something sinister. "Race card" is one of those wordplays guaranteed to generate media noise. In Obama's case, it was his predicting the future based on the past—that the Republican argument against his candidacy (and his problem was that he called out McCain by name) would be to make voters afraid of him. They would talk about his "funny name," Obama told an audience in Missouri, say he's not patriotic, claim he was too risky. "You know, he doesn't look like all those other presidents on those dollar bills, you know."

Simple translation, and no surprise: He's not a white man.

There was a telling moment in the campaign shortly after Obama wrapped up the nomination. He had gathered many of his volunteers and staff at Chicago headquarters to thank them—and to remind them of all they had been through together. He mentioned the mistakes he had made, and the skepticism and cynicism they all had confronted about his candidacy. There was a "good heart to this campaign," he continued. After noting the single mothers struggling without health care, the towns that are dying because of chronic job loss, the people he encountered who are concerned about global warming, Darfur, and education, Obama lowered the boom: "We don't have an option now."

Moments like these hardly ever come around, Obama told his troops. The whole country was depending on them. He reminded them of that first victory in Iowa. If we hadn't won there, he said, another Democrat would have emerged and we'd all be out on the trail now campaigning and volunteering for some other candidate. "But because we won, we now have no choice. We have to win."

He was pumping them up—to make history, beat McCain, "change the world." As the applause grew, Obama decided that was enough. He had made the case. It was time to exit. Get some rest, he told the troops, but come back fired up.

"I love you guys," he said. "Let's go win the election."

—Kevin Merida

About the Author

Kevin Merida is an associate editor at the *Washington Post*. He has covered or supervised the coverage of six presidential campaigns, including the 2008 contest. In 2000, he was named Journalist of the Year by the National Association of Black Journalists. He is the author of the critically acclaimed and prizewinning *Supreme Discomfort: The Divided Soul of Clarence Thomas*. He lives in Maryland.

Photography credits

Page 1: Obama speaks to a crowd estimated at 75,000 during a rally at Waterfront Park in Portland, Oregon, May 18, 2008. It was one of the largest crowds anyone could remember a presidential candidate ever drawing for a single event. © 2008 Getty Images-Justin Sullivan

Pages 2–3: Photographic series shows Barack Obama and his wife, Michelle, onstage during his election night rally at the Xcel Energy Center in St. Paul, Minnesota, at the end of the 2008 Democratic party primaries, June 3, 2008. © Emmanuel Dunand/AFP/Getty Images

Page 4: Obama walks back to his office on Capitol Hill after a series of votes on the Senate Floor, May 13, 2008. © Tim Sloan/AFP/Getty Images

Page 7: Barack Obama in his Chicago home office. © Annie Leibovitz/Contact Press Images, originally photographed for *Men's Vogue*

Page 9: Senator Barack Obama (D-IL), his wife, Michelle, and daughters. © Annie Leibovitz/Contact Press Images, originally photographed for *Vanity Fair*

Pages 10–11: Obama delivers a speech during a rally at the Fort Worth Convention Center. © Vernon Bryant/Dallas Morning News

Page 12: After an Obama event in Corpus Christi, Texas. © Peter Slevin

Page 13 top: © CJ Gunther/epa/Corbis

Page 13 bottom: © Larry W. Smith/epa/Corbis

Page 14: August 16, 2007. © Joshua Lott/Reuters/Corbis

Page 15: © Rick Friedman/Corbis

Page 16: © Brooks Kraft/Corbis

Page 17: © 2008 Bill Pugliano/Getty Images

Page 19: Obama delivers a speech at Apostolic Church of God speaking about the importance of fathers being involved in the raising of their children. Chicago, Illinois, June 15, 2008. © David Banks/Getty Images

Page 20 top: Democratic presidential hopeful Senator Barack Obama jogs off the stage after speaking in Mitchell, South Dakota, June 1, 2008. © Rick Wilking/Reuters/Corbis

Page 20 bottom: Democratic presidential hopefuls Senator John Edwards of North Carolina and Senator Hillary Clinton of New York listen as Senator Barack Obama of Illinois answers a question during the Democratic debate at Saint Anselm College, June 3, 2007. © CJ Gunther/Pool/epa/Corbis

Page 21: Obama waves to supporters during a rally at Nissan Pavilion, June 5, 2008. © AFP/Getty Images/Mandel Ngan

Page 22: © Chip Somodevilla/Getty Images

Page 23 top: Various campaign buttons for sale at a campaign rally where television talk-show host Oprah Winfey endorsed Obama. Des Moines, Iowa, December 8, 2007. © Michal Czerwonka/epa/Corbis

Page 23 bottom: Democratic presidential hopeful Senator Barack Obama shakes hands at the Clark County Government Center during a campaign stop in Las Vegas, February 18, 2007. © Christopher Farina/Corbis

Page 24: Supporters of Democratic presidential candidate Senator Barack Obama cheer as Obama arrives at his South Dakota and Montana presidential primary election night rally at the Xcel Energy Center in St. Paul, Minnesota, June 3, 2008. © Jason Reed/Reuters/Corbis

Pages 26–27: Senator Barack Obama leaves the White House after a meeting with U.S. president George W. Bush and members of Congress, January 5, 2007. © Jim Young/X90065/Reuters/Corbis

Page 28: © Jim Young/Reuters/Corbis

Page 29: Michelle Obama attends a fund-raiser for her husband, Democratic presidential candidate Senator Barack Obama (D-IL), at designer Calvin Klein's home in New York City, June 17, 2008. © Marcel Thomas/FilmMagic

Page 30: Supporters for Democratic presidential hopeful Senator Barack Obama rally, before the CNN/*Los Angeles Times* Democratic presidential debate, at the Kodak Theater in Hollywood. © Ted Soqui/Ted Soqui Photography USA/Corbis

Page 31 top: Paoli, Pennsylvania. © Scout Tufankjian/Polaris

Page 31 bottom: Wayne, Pennsylvania. © Scout Tufankjian/Polaris

Page 32: © Chip Somodevilla/Getty Images

Page 33: © Tim Sloan/AFP/Getty Images

Page 34 top: Photograph by Marvin Nicholson from the collection of Seith Mann, February 1, 2008.

Page 34 bottom: Obama delivers campaign remarks to a large crowd inside the St. Pete Times Forum. Tampa, Florida, May 21, 2008. © Charles Ommanney/Getty Images

Page 35 top: Supporters of Democratic presidential hopeful Senator Barack Obama (D-IL) wait for him to arrive at an election night rally at the Xcel Energy Center in St. Paul, Minnesota, June 3, 2008. © Scott Olson/Getty Images

Page 35 bottom: A woman reaches to take a photograph of Democratic presidential hopeful Senator Barack Obama (D-IL) as he speaks at a town-hall meeting in a show barn at the Pennington County Event Center in Rapid City, South Dakota, May 31, 2008. © Chip Somodevilla/Getty Images

Page 36 top: May 31, 2008. © Chip Somodevilla/Getty Images

Page 36 bottom: May 31, 2008. © Chip Somodevilla/Getty Images

Page 37: The amateur hula dance troupe, the Obama Girls, shout "Yes we can!" during a rally to support U.S. Democratic presidential hopeful Senator Barack Obama in Japan's city of Obama, Fukui prefecture, on May 21, 2008, after Obama declared he was "within reach" of the nomination in the Democratic White House race. © Toru Yamanaka/AFP/Getty Images

Page 38: Democratic U.S. presidential candidate Senator Barack Obama (D-IL) waves after speaking at the 2008 American Israel Public Affairs Committee (AIPAC) Policy Conference at the Washington Convention Center in Washington, D.C., June 4, 2008. © Justin Sullivan/Getty Images

Page 39: Presidential candidate Senator Barack Obama speaks to supporters at a lakeside rally in downtown Austin where 20,000-plus people hear him speak. © Bob Daemmrich/Corbis

Page 40 top: The exterior of the Farmers for Obama headquarters in Vincennes, Indiana, around 2:45 A.M. on Tuesday, May 6, 2008, after it was vandalized by persons unknown. Windows were broken and "hate messages" were spray-painted on the facade. Photo was taken and provided by a farmer and Obama volunteer who was made aware of the vandalism right after it happened; shortly thereafter it was cleaned up. © Ray McCormick

Page 40 bottom: © Bob Daemmrich/Corbis

Page 42 top: Supporters pass out bumper stickers for Democratic presidential candidate Senator Barack Obama prior to a campaign appearance at the University of New Hampshire, February 12, 2007. © Brooks Kraft/Corbis

Page 42 bottom: Senator Barack Obama and his wife, Michelle, arrive to vote in the Super Tuesday primary at Beulah Shoesmith Elementary School in Chicago, Illinois, February 5, 2008. © Preston Keres/TWP

Page 43 top: Senator Barack Obama signs a copy of Time magazine with his picture on the cover, while visiting KGO studios for an interview on the Ronn Owens radio program, October 25, 2006. © Michael Macor/San Francisco Chronicle/Corbis

Page 43 bottom: Obama in a George Washington Carver School classroom, with students and teachers, New Orleans. © David Burnett (Contact Press Images)

Page 44: Aboard private plane briefing reporters en route to New Orleans, Louisiana, February 7, 2008. © David Burnett (Contact Press Images)

Page 45: Participants at a rally marking Martin Luther King Day in Columbia, South Carolina. Three Democratic presidential candidates, Illinois senator Barack Obama, New York senator Hillary Clinton, and former North Carolina senator John Edwards took part in the event prior to the South Carolina Democratic debate happening later in the day. © Michal Czerwonka/epa/Corbis

Page 46: Democratic presidential candidate Barack Obama at a town hall with veterans in San Antonio, Texas. Obama wears a bracelet bearing the name of Sgt. Ryan David Jopek, killed in action on August 2, 2006. © Linda Davidson/TWP

Page 47: Michelle Obama looks on as Senator Barack Obama gives his Super Tuesday election night speech in Chicago, February 5, 2008. © Preston Keres/TWP

Page 48: Senator Barack Obama holds a rally at the Izod Center in Meadowlands, New Jersey, on the eve of Super Tuesday, February 4, 2008. © Preston Keres/TWP

Page 49: A Barack Obama staffer displays her necklace of "Obama" in Scrabble tiles at a campaign event in Waterloo, Iowa, December 15, 2007. © Scout Tufankjian/Polaris

Page 50: Democratic presidential candidate Barack Obama and wife, Michelle, hold an outdoor primary-night party in San Antonio, March 4, 2008. © Linda Davidson/TWP

Page 53: Obama holds a rally at the Kentucky International Convention Center in Louisville. © Jahi Chikwendiu/TWP

Page 54 top: March 1, 2008. © Linda Davidson/TWP

Page 54 bottom: © Linda Davidson/TWP

Page 55: Democratic presidential candidate Senator Barack Obama makes an unscheduled stop at George's Pizza & Steak, between campaign stops. © Steve Pope/epa/Corbis

Pages 56–57: Senator Barack Obama greets supporters at Pamela's P&G Restaurant in Pittsburgh on the day of Pennsylvania's Democratic presidential primary election, April 22, 2008. © Jahi Chikwendiu/TWP

Pages 58–59: 2008 © David Burnett (Contact Press Images)

Page 60: Democratic presidential hopeful Senator Barack Obama waits to speak in Aberdeen, South Dakota. © Rick Wilking/Reuters/Corbis

Page 61: Democratic presidential candidate and U.S. senator Barack Obama holds a rally. © Melina Mara/TWP

Page 62: A woman holds a child at a Houston rally for Obama two days prior to the Texas primary and caucuses, March 2, 2008. © Bob Gore

Page 63: Obama supporter Chalonda Marcus of Forney cries as the Democratic presidential hopeful delivers a speech at a rally at the Reunion Arena in Dallas, February 20, 2008. © Vernon Bryant/Dallas Morning

Pages 64–65: Stevie Wonder performs at a rally hosted by Michelle Obama for her husband, Democratic presidential hopeful Senator Barack Obama, at the Pauley Pavilion at UCLA, as guest speakers (3rd left to right) Oprah Winfrey, Maria Elena Durazo, and Caroline Kennedy Schlossberg, daughter of JFK, listen, February 3, 2008. © Ted Soqui/Ted Soqui Photography USA/Corbis

Page 66: © Tannen Maury/epa/Corbis

Page 67: Democratic presidential candidate Senator Barack Obama wipes sweat from his brow as he signs autographs after taking part in the Democratic presidential debate at Howard University. © Kevin Lamarque/Reuters/Corbis

Page 68: Hands of supporters reach out to touch Democratic presidential candidate Barack Obama during the final election-night rally at the Xcel Energy Center in St. Paul, Minnesota, at the end of the 2008 Democratic party primaries, June 3, 2008. © Emmanuel Dunand/AFP/Getty Images

Page 69 top: Democratic presidential hopeful Senator Barack Obama signs autographs following a Democratic debate with New York senator and Democratic presidential hopeful Hillary Clinton, held at the Wolstein Center on the campus of Cleveland State University, February 26, 2008. © David Maxwell/epa/Corbis

Page 69 bottom: Supporters listen to Democratic presidential hopeful Senator Barack Obama of Illinois, as he campaigns at Pennsylvania State University's Greater Allegheny campus, April 21, 2008. © Matthew Cavanaugh/epa/Corbis

Page 70: A look at how younger people use the Internet to organize and gather political support for presidential candidates. Specifically, we focus on participants in Facebook.com at Iowa State University who volunteer for Barack Obama's campaign rally and others who just come. Students, teachers, and locals alike clamored to get a handshake and autograph from Obama after the speech. © Linda Davidson/TWP

Page 71: People shake hands with Democratic presidential hopeful U.S. senator Barack Obama (D-IL) during a Broward County campaign rally at the BankAtlantic Center in Sunrise, Florida, May 23, 2008. © Joe Raedle/Getty Images

Page 72: Presidential hopeful Senator Barack Obama (D-IL) speaks to a crowd of supporters in a church in post–Hurricane Katrina New Orleans, July 21, 2006. © Will Steacy

Page 73: Democratic presidential hopeful Senator Barack Obama (D-IL) holds a town-hall meeting at the Aberdeen Civic Arena in Aberdeen, South Dakota, May 31, 2008. Obama later held a news conference to discuss the DNC's decision to seat the delegates from Florida and Michigan at the national convention and to talk about his family's resignation as members of Trinity United Church of Christ in Chicago. © Chip Somodevilla/Getty Images

Pages 74–75: Democratic presidential candidate U.S. senator Barack Obama and his wife, Michelle, celebrate during his election-night rally at the Xcel Energy Center in St. Paul, Minnesota, at the end of the 2008 Democratic Party primaries, June 3, 2008. © Emmanuel Dunand/AFP/Getty Images

Pages 76–77: Democratic presidential hopeful U.S. senator Barack Obama (D-IL) and his wife, Michelle, greet the crowd during a rally at Waterfront Park in Portland, Oregon, May 18, 2008. © Justin Sullivan/Getty Images

Pages 78–79: Democratic presidential candidate Senator Barack Obama talks on the phone with his family during a campaign bus trip near Sioux City, Iowa. © Carlos Barria/Reuters/Corbis

Page 80: Obama became the candidate of young people this campaign season. Here, a young supporter looks on as the candidate addresses the largest rally of his campaign, at Waterfront Park in Portland, Oregon, May 18, 2008. © Justin Sullivan/Getty Images

Page 81: Democratic presidential hopeful Senator Barack Obama and his wife, Michelle, acknowledge the crowd during a rally at the Nashua South High School in Nashua, New Hampshire, after Obama conceded in the New Hampshire primary, January 8, 2008. © CJ Gunther/epa/Corbis

Page 82: Senator Barack Obama campaigns in New Orleans, Louisiana, speaking at Tulane University. Afterward, posing for pictures in front of a Tulane basketball mural, February 7, 2008. © David Burnett (Contact Press Images)

Page 83: U.S. presidential hopeful Barack Obama plays in a 3-on-3 basketball game with his staffer Reggie Love (not seen) looking on. © Yana Paskova

Page 84: Democratic presidential hopeful Senator Barack Obama appears with Massachusetts senator John Kerry during a rally at the College of Charleston. © Erik S. Lesser/epa/Corbis

Page 87: Presidential candidate Senator Barack Obama (L) greets former president Bill Clinton after a reenactment of the 1965 Selma-to-Montgomery march. © Brooks Kraft/Corbis

Page 88: © Terrence Jennings

Page 89: © Stefan Zaklin/epa/Corbis

Page 91: Democratic presidential hopeful Senator Barack Obama with Senator Ted Kennedy backstage before a rally at American University in Washington, D.C. Also backstage is Caroline Kennedy Schlossberg, daughter of the late president John F. Kennedy. Senator Kennedy announced his endorsement of Senator Obama for president, January 28, 2008. © Brooks Kraft/Corbis

Page 92 top: Barack Obama rallies New York at Washington Square Park, September 27, 2007. © Terrence Jennings

Page 92 bottom: © 2007 Marc Piscotty

Page 93 top: © Michal Czerwonka

Page 93 bottom: Barack Obama at Time Warner's Conversations on the Circle, July 24, 2007. © Timothy Greenfield Sanders

Page 94: Democratic presidential candidates Barack Obama and Hillary Clinton come (separately) to Selma to commemorate the civil rights movement and reenactment of the march across the Edmund Pettus Bridge, March 4, 2007. © Linda Davidson/TWP

Page 96: Senator and Democratic presidential candidate Chris Dodd and Senator and Democratic presidential candidate Barack Obama react to audience members after the Iowa Brown and Black Forum. © Steve Pope/epa/Corbis

Page 97 top: Former NFL Dallas Cowboys running back Emmitt Smith speaks about Democratic presidential hopeful Senator Barack Obama during a rally at Reunion Arena in Dallas, Texas. © Larry W. Smith/epa/Corbis

Page 97 bottom: A person holds pictures of Democratic presidential hopefuls Senator Hillary Clinton and Senator Barack Obama during a Clinton campaign event at the University of Miami, Florida. © Carlos Barria/Reuters/Corbis

Page 98: Democratic presidential hopeful Barack Obama makes his way onto the stage for a rally at Nissan Pavilion in Bristow, Virginia, June 5, 2008. © Mandel Ngan/AFP/Getty Images

Page 99: © Chip Somodevilla/Getty Images

Page 100 top: July 3, 2008. © Katherine S. Carey

Page 100 bottom: © Thomas Dworzak/Magnum Photos

Page 101: May 31, 2008. © Chip Somodevilla/Getty Images

Page 102: © Lea Suzuki/San Francisco

Page 103: © Gordon J. Davis

Page 104: Father Michael Pfleger (L) and the Reverend Jesse Jackson (R) attend an anti-gun rally outside the manufacturing facilities of D. S. Arms in Barrington, Illinois, August 28, 2007. Pfleger is under fire for mocking Democratic presidential candidate Senator Hillary Clinton (D-NY) during a racially charged speech at Democratic presidential candidate Senator Barack Obama's (D-IL) Chicago church. © Scott Olson/Getty Images

Page 105: The Reverend Dr. Jeremiah A. Wright, Jr., speaks at the NAACP's 53rd Annual Fight for Freedom Fund Dinner at Cobo Hall in Detroit, Michigan. © Jeff Kowalsky/epa/Corbis

Page 106: May 14, 2007. © Chris Williams Photography

Page 107: © Spencer Platt/Getty Images

Page 108: Oprah Winfrey speaks during a campaign rally for Democratic presidential candidate Senator Barack Obama at the 11,000-seat Verizon Wireless Arena. © Jodi Hilton/Corbis

Page 109: The crowd waiting in line at the Avenue nightclub to get into a fund-raising party for the Obama campaign, September 28, 2007. © Michel du Cille/TWP

Page 110: The cover of Time magazine features a portrait of American politician and Democratic presidential hopeful Barack Obama accompanied by the caption "And the Winner Is . . . (Really, we're pretty sure this time)," May 19, 2008. © Callie Shell-Aurora/Time & Life Pictures/Getty Images

Page 111 top left: July 10, 2008. © RollingStone Magazine/Wenner Media

Page 111 top right: September 1, 2007. © VIBE Magazine

Page 111 bottom left: January 2008. © Lonnie C. Major/Black Enterprise/Vistalux

Page 111 bottom right: Reprinted with permission of The Onion © 2008 by Onion, Inc.

Page 112: © Phil Masturzo/TWP

Page 113: Senator Barack Obama (D-IL) during a town-hall-style meeting at Kennedy High School with the residents of Cedar Rapids, Iowa, February 11, 2007. © Jason Reed/Reuters/Corbis

Page 114: New York Women for Obama rally in Central Park, New York, February 5, 2008. © Alice Dear

Page 115: (Left to right) Gloria Dulan-Wilson, Alice Dear, and Joy Wellington, New York City, February 5, 2008. © Alice Dear

Page 117: Collection of Montez Martin. © Montez Martin

Page 118 top: July 7, 2008. © Peter Wynn Thompson/The New York Times/Redux

Page 118 bottom: July 7, 2008. © Doug Mills/The New York Times/Redux

Page 119: March 3, 2008. © Linda Davidson/TWP

Page 121: Barack Obama and Hillary Clinton talk on the plane on their way to the Unity rally in Unity, New Hampshire. © Linda Davidson/TWP

Page 122: © Jahi Chikwendiu/TWP

Page 123: 2007. © Thomas Dworzak/Magnum Photos

Pages 124–25: Supporters fawn over Barack Obama as he holds a baby for its mother's photo op. © Linda Davidson/TWP

Page 126: © Michel du Cille/TWP

Page 127: Senator Barack Obama at a campaign event. © Eli Reed/Magnum Photos

Page 128: Senator Barack Obama answers a question during the Q & A portion of the NALEO program, June 28, 2008. © Linda Davidson/TWP

Page 129: Senator Barack Obama stands with his Massachusetts support group, February 4, 2008. © Preston Keres/TWP

Page 130: Chelsea Clinton and her father, former U.S. president Bill Clinton (L), look on as Senator Hillary Rodham Clinton (D-NY) greets supporters at the National Building Museum, June 7, 2008. © Justin Sullivan/Getty Images

Page 131: U.S. Speaker of the House Nancy Pelosi (D-CA) and Democratic National Committee chairman Howard Dean listen during a news conference at DNC headquarters in Washington, D.C., June 10, 2008. © Alex Wong/Getty Images

Page 133: Senator Hillary Clinton speaks to supporters at the National Building Museum in Washington, D.C., June 7, 2008. On Saturday Clinton threw her full support and energy behind Barack Obama, as she endorsed the Democratic White House nominee and vowed to do all she could to send him to the White House. © Mandel Ngan/AFP/Getty Images

Page 134: © Chip Somodevilla/Getty Images

Page 135 top: © Frank Polich/Reuters/Corbis

Page 135 bottom: © Brooks Kraft/Corbis

Page 136: Democratic presidential candidate Senator Barack Obama (D-IL) and former U.S. vice president Al Gore appear onstage together after Gore endorsed him at a rally at Joe Louis Arena © Bill Pugliano/Getty Images

Page 137: Kenya's newspapers are displayed in the streets of Nairobi on June 5, 2008, after Democratic presidential candidate Senator Barack Obama's nomination victory places him a heartbeat away from the White House. © Simon Maina/AFP/ Getty Images

Pages 138–139: © Brooks Kraft/Corbis

Page 140: February 10, 2007, Senator Barack Obama waves to spectators as he arrives to announce his candidacy for president of the United States at the Old State Capitol in Springfield, Illinois. © Associated Press

Page 143: Democratic presidential hopefuls Barack Obama and Hillary Clinton laugh during the Democratic debates in Las Vegas, Nevada, January 15, 2008. © Andrew Gombert/epa/Corbis

Page 144: Senator Barack Obama, Democratic contender for the presidential nomination, campaigns in Omaha, Nebraska. At the Omaha Civic Center, he speaks first to an overflow crowd of about 500, and then to 10,000 in the big arena. Here, he walks through the basement of the Civic Center en route to the overflow crowd while on his cell phone, February 7, 2008. © David Burnett (Contact Press Images)

Page 145: Senator Barack Obama wins the Iowa primary and speaks to supporters, January 3, 2008. © Melina Mara/TWP

Page 149: Locals listen to U.S. Senator Barack Obama speak outside the courthouse in Manning, South Carolina, November 2, 2007. © Callie Shell/Aurora Photos

Page 151: Barack and Michelle Obama embrace at a rally after he was narrowly defeated in the New Hampshire primary, January 8, 2008. © Scout Tufankjian/Polaris

Page 154: Democratic presidential hopeful Senator Barack Obama (D-IL) participates in a church service before giving a speech about fatherhood at the Apostolic Church of God, June 15, 2008. © David Banks/Getty Images

Page 158: Peace, Change, Hope, Obama. Man with Obama haircut stopped for a photo op on the street, July 2008. © Jessica Ingram

Page 160: Senator Barack Obama boards his campaign plane in Pittsburgh, en route to Philadelphia on the day of Pennsylvania's Democratic presidential primary election, April 22, 2008. © Jahi Chikwendiu/TWP

For my mom, Ruth Willis—DW

For my wife, Donna Britt—KM

✧   ✧   ✧

ACKNOWLEDGMENTS

Every project needs a creator. We thank Dawn Davis, editorial director of HarperCollins's Amistad imprint, for having the vision to see this book and for bringing us together in this beautiful collaboration. Heather Hart, Christina Morgan, Jane Lusaka, Leslie Willis-Lowry, Hank Willis Thomas, Faith Childs, and Andrew Blauner provided invaluable support. The production team at HarperCollins worked gracefully under pressure.

We also thank Michel du Cille, the top photo editor at the *Washington Post*, for culling and sharing the wonderful work of the paper's photography staff. Other *Post* friends and colleagues generously shared their thoughts about Obama and provided consultation during the writing and editing process. Notable among them are Peter Slevin, who offered a remarkable photo of enthusiastic Obama supporters from his personal collection, and Mike Fletcher. Thanks also to Sarah Lewis, the staff of the department of Photography and Imaging at NYU, Chris Bernstein, the Leica Gallery, Michael Shulmann, Rachelle Brown, Jeanne Moutoussamy Ashe, Katie Walker, and Jessica Martin.

Finally, and most important, we thank our families for their love and support: Kevin's wife, Donna Britt, and sons, Skye, Darrell, and Hamani. We also are grateful to George and Doris Hill, Kevin's pop and mom, for lifting us up and providing space at their home in Maryland to work on this project.

✧   ✧   ✧

OBAMA: THE HISTORIC CAMPAIGN IN PHOTOGRAPHS. Copyright © 2008 by Kevin Merida and Deborah Willis. All rights reserved. Printed in the United States of America. No part of this book may be used or reproduced in any manner whatsoever without written permission except in the case of brief quotations embodied in critical articles and reviews. For information address HarperCollins Publishers, 10 East 53rd Street, New York, NY 10022.

HarperCollins books may be purchased for educational, business, or sales promotional use. For information please write: Special Markets Department, HarperCollins Publishers, 10 East 53rd Street, New York, NY 10022.

FIRST EDITION

Designed by Laura Klynstra

Library of Congress Cataloging-in-Publication Data has been applied for.

ISBN 978-0-06-173309-3

08 09 10 11 12 ID/RRD 10 9 8 7 6 5 4